3-11
V 3-12

SOUTHERN BOUQUETS

SOUTHERN BOUQUETS

Melissa Bigner with Heather Barrie

Photography by Peter Frank Edwards

GIBBS SMITH

TO ENRICH AND INSPIRE HUMANKIND

Salt Lake City | Charleston | Santa Fe | Santa Barbara

First Edition
14 13 12 11 10   5 4 3 2

Text © 2010 Melissa Bigner
Photographs © 2010 Peter Frank Edwards

Published by
Gibbs Smith
P.O. Box 667
Layton, Utah 84041

1.800.835.4993 orders
www.gibbs-smith.com

Printed and bound in Hong Kong
Gibbs Smith books are printed on paper produced from sustainable PEFC-certified forest/controlled wood source.
Learn more at: www.pefc.org"

Library of Congress Cataloging-in-Publication Data

Bigner, Melissa.
Southern bouquets / Melissa Bigner with Heather Barrie ; photographs by Peter Frank Edwards. — 1st ed.
     p. cm.
ISBN-13: 978-1-4236-0507-2
ISBN-10: 1-4236-0507-1
1. Bouquets—Southern states. 2. Flowers—Collection and preservation—Southern states. I. Barrie, Heather. II. Title.
SB449.5.B65B54 2010
745.920975—dc22
                                                     2009033700

Heartfelt thanks to everyone—and everything—that nurtured each bloom, branch, and blade onto these pages.

CONTENTS

INTRODUCTION

In Hampton Park, a few streets over from where I live in Charleston, South Carolina,

winding paths of primly raked, shell-laden sand meander past beds of Noisette

roses, Mexican petunias, stipa grass, and more blooms than you can imagine.

Iron lampposts rise from the ground alongside heirloom camellias, crepe myrtles,

and azaleas, each in so many varieties an encyclopedia could barely keep up with

the naming. In the wide-open stretches, magnolias mingle with long-leaf pines,

live oaks, cypress, firs, sycamores, palmettos, and dogwoods alike. Something is

always blooming there, casting enticing scents and eye-catching colors, and, like

me, scores of reverent people flock to the park in the fresh hours of the day to revel

in the lot of it.

On one morning's jog there, I got to thinking about the park's flowers and how flora touches us here in the South. Look around old homesteads, and even if only the foundation still stands, there's sure to be a garden growing on, effortlessly stunning and wildly romantic. In my neighborhood—politely called a "transitional" area—I come across centenarian houses that are falling in on themselves, but at their feet, hydrangeas grin, naked ladies dance, daffodils show their brave faces, wisteria sigh, and spiderworts wink at passersby. Someone once mothered these plants, and now folks like me are reaping the benefits.

And while no one I know full-on plunders the gardens of occupied houses or decimates the well-populated beds of public parks, the majority of us do partake in a little judicious clipping, be it from common ground, shall I say, or from our own yards. Down here, it's as common for dinner guests to gift a handful of fresh azalea blooms, a box of camellia heads, or a cluster of daffodils as it is for them to show up with a bottle of wine. No matter how humble the bloom, the flowers are received in gushing fashion and given a place of honor at the gathering. And it's not just a special event thing, either. I swear, I can't remember ever going to my Mom's house without seeing some such vestige of a friend's visit or some little blossom in a tiny chipped pitcher enlivening this or that corner of her rooms. These arrangements are not fussy, nor do they typically feature fussy plants. They are simple bouquets—simple, fresh Southern bouquets.

So thanks to that jog, this book came about, to celebrate old Southern blooms, how they color our homes and connect us to the good green earth. I teamed with Charleston floral designer Heather Barrie and we made a pact to gather blooms from our own yards, from friends'

gardens, from abandoned lots, from local parks and plantations (with permission, of course), from small area farms and even from country ditches. Our goal? To stay away from florists' refrigerators and stay true to a "real" look born of the garden bouquets we love.

As for the "Southernness" of the flora, well, no, the flowers we picked are not restricted to those states below the Mason-Dixon line. But they are the ones that haunt our days, fill our childhood memories—mine from North Carolina and Heather's from Georgia. Common to our varied landscapes, they thus merited inclusion. And if you're looking for a favorite that's not headlining as a chapter, poke around a bit. Cherished stars such as gardenias, lilies, irises, and magnolias pop up as supporting cast members here and there.

Lastly, I'm by no means a Latin-spouting gardener, and in some cases, our flower donors didn't even know the names of their treasures. So while I've done my best to identify the various blooms we've included—thanks to a host of regional experts—sometimes we simply were all in the dark and had to call the questionable variety a "found" flower. But I think that's forgivable since this book was never intended to be a plant catalog.

Rather, it's my hope that the stories we've collected, the alluring bouquets Heather fashioned, and the romantic photos that lensman (and green-thumb guru) Peter Frank Edwards captured will uplift anyone who peruses our little book. These flowers, after all, their resilience and beauty, are marvels pure, fresh, and simple.

—Melissa Bigner

CAMELLIAS

COMMON NAME: Camellia

COMMON BOTANICAL NAMES: *Camellia japonica* and *C. sasanqua*

PLANT TYPE: Evergreen shrub

FLOWER COLORS: Pink, red, variegated, and white

ORIGINS: China, Japan, and Southeast Asia

IDEAL GROWING CONDITIONS: Partial sun; well-drained but moist and acidic soil

SIZE: 8 to 15 feet tall, 6 feet wide

ZONES: 7 to 10

BLOOMING TIME: September through April. *Sasanquas* bloom in late fall through early winter, and *japonicas* follow in late winter through spring.

ARRANGING TIPS: Cut blooms with as much of the woody stem attached as possible and choose buds that are just barely cracking open to allow the petals to unfurl over the course of several days. When blooms droop, trim stems away and float heads in a bowl of water.

VASE LIFE: Four days to one week

MEANINGS: Evanescence and long-lasting love

TRIVIA: Renowned French botanist André Michaux is credited with introducing outdoor-thriving camellias to America via Charleston, South Carolina, in 1786. Drawn to the Lowcountry for its temperate climate, Michaux spent a decade tending to his experimental gardens in the Goose Creek area. While there, he gifted several of these camellias to friends at Middleton Place Plantation and soon the shrubs spread throughout the region. • By the mid-1800s, major collections thrived in the South—there were some 300 varieties at Charleston's Magnolia Plantation alone—and a significant camellia nursery was established in Augusta, Georgia. • Today, many of those early camellias still grow on the grounds of Middleton amid more than 2,000 newer varieties, and Magnolia's gardens are still rich with the plants as well. • Camellias are the state flower of Alabama and the city flower of Slidell, Louisiana.

To ensure tiny bud vases don't topple under the weight of a bloom, place pebbles in the base of the vessel. 'Pink Perfection' was brought to Europe from Japan in 1875 and has long been a Southern favorite, as the 10- to 12-foot shrub can flower well into the spring in warmer zones. Eudora Welty's Jackson, Mississippi, home boasts some forty camellia bushes, including this variety *(facing)*. Deep windowsills make a dream spot for bud vases, but know that sunlight speeds up their demise, and that dappled light or shade is best for cut flowers, unless you're trying to force blooms open. The blue and gold of these Russian vessels contrast sweetly with the white blossom of a semi-double camellia, so-called for its two rows of petals *(right)*.

SOUTHERN STORY: A CARE PACKAGE

Back in the 1940s, Eleanor Ilderton was the first of her family's generation to leave Charleston, South Carolina's Lowcountry when she married and moved to High Point, North Carolina. And though her new city was a mere state away, it was a world apart from Eleanor's childhood haunts, such as Fenwick Hall Plantation, where she used to visit her Aunt Nellie. A sprawling estate on a sea island, Fenwick Hall was known for its prolific spread of live oaks and sea of lush camellias; by comparison, Eleanor's first Tarheel garden inevitably came up short.

Nevertheless, the ambitious young woman and a host of new girlfriends founded their own little garden club named the Garden Makers. But when it came time for Eleanor to host, her fledgling flowerbeds and still-stumpy shrubs had yielded little-to-no homegrown blooms to dress the house for the gathering. Somehow, back home in Charleston, Aunt Nellie caught wind of the coming party and rallied Eleanor's mother.

"Carrie," Aunt Nellie supposedly said to her sister, "we've got to get that child some camellias." The two set upon Fenwick's legendary flora,

cutting bloom after prize bloom. They took their bounty to Nellie's kitchen and floated the camellia heads in cool water while they cut several raw potatoes into wedges so they could easily drive the flower stems into the tubers' flesh. With the blooms thus rooted, the pair started sewing the camellias to the base of the box with thread and needle so as to secure them in place.

When the box was brimming, the sisters tucked Spanish moss around the heads and lightly watered the lot of it to keep the flowers fresh. They covered the blooms with a layer of wax paper, tied the box with twine, addressed it, and drove the whole thing to the bus station, where they bought it a one-way ticket to High Point.

"I can't tell you how exciting it was to head to the station here to see what they had been up to," says Eleanor, remembering the times when instant communication equaled a party phone line at best and packages were a lifeline. Needless to say, the homegrown blooms were the hit at that Garden Makers meeting. And since then, just as Eleanor eventually came into her own, so did her camellias.

Cluster a collection of smaller vessels to create the illusion of an abundant centerpiece. When choosing bouquet bedfellows, look to what's blooming at the same time; paperwhites and *Camellia japonicas* both show their faces in late winter *(facing)*. If you can't clip much stem, or if your camellias are on the way out, fill a bowl with cool water and float the heads in it to extend their "shelf life." As for this vessel? It's a $3 thrift-store find *(right)*.

BEHIND THE SCENES

Sometimes you have to look no farther than your own backyard to find a trove of stunning blooms. To gather the winning camellias seen here, Heather and I had to look just a little farther, into our neighbors' backyards.

First we headed to the James Island, South Carolina, home of Peter Frank Edwards, who photographed this book. Frank moved into his 1950s ranch a few years ago, and when the cool air hits, scores of sixty-year-old camellias bloom. Towering up to a story high and tucked under a canopy of live oaks, Frank's camellias are so wild and lush that they dominate the half-acre lot with their glossy evergreen leaves, plump blooms, and frilly blossoms.

After loading our buckets there, we headed about five minutes away to an oak-lined street that deadends at Wappoo Creek, a meandering but powerful waterway that cuts through the marshes clinging to the edges of Charleston. There, we found Kristin and Chris Newman's stone-faced cottage, which, like Frank's home, came with its own decades-old Eden. Every last one of their camellia shrubs drooped under the pregnant weight of pale white, soft pink, and flecked heads, and by morning's end, the flower van and the gray winter day were all the brighter for their colorful show. In the wake of the shoot at my mother's French Quarter home, we left her a trail of bouquets, and January there has never been so vibrant.

Leave glossy evergreen camellia leaves on the stem to provide a colorful contrast to the soft texture and palette of petals. Showy blooms like camellias make for great single-stemmed bouquets. The variegation seen in camellias is often a result of a common virus or genetics *(facing)*.

Allow a bouquet to be a little unruly and asymmetrical and it mimics the organic beauty of a naturally growing plant.

'C.M. Hovey' 1853

'C.M. Wilson' 1949

'Jessie Gale' 1958

'Professor Charles S. Sargent' 1925

'Cup of Beauty' 1848

'Spring Sonnet' 1951

'Ville de Nantes' 1910

'Pink Perfection' 1875

DAFFODILS

COMMON NAMES AND TYPES: Daffodil, jonquil, and paperwhite

COMMON BOTANICAL NAME: *Narcissus, N. jonquilla,* and *N. tazetta*

PLANT TYPE: Perennial (bulb)

FLOWER COLORS: Bicolor, cream, orange, pale pink, white, and yellow

ORIGINS: Asia and Europe

IDEAL GROWING CONDITIONS: Full sun to partial shade; moist but well-drained soil. Let a month-and-a-half pass after blooming before you remove foliage to ensure growth the following year.

SIZE: 4 to 20 inches tall

ZONES: 3 to 9

BLOOMING TIME: Late winter through spring

ARRANGING TIPS: Try not to get the sap on your skin, as it's an irritant. Cut stems on an angle to help them best drink water. Change water and trim stems daily, as the sap thwarts longevity.

VASE LIFE: Three to six days

MEANING: Rebirth

TRIVIA: In the 1930s, one group of the Civilian Conservation Corps planted thousands of daffodil bulbs at Tennessee's Cades Cove in a pattern that spelled out the name of their company—the 5427th. Visit March to April to see their handiwork today. • Franklin, Tennessee's Carton Plantation is home to a massive spread of pre-1869 daffodils. Cultivated as a tribute to the first blooming flowers wounded Confederate soldiers recuperating there would have seen, the narcissus are as much a memorial to the past as are the 1,500 military headstones on the grounds. • The Daniels of Camden, Arkansas, and their "backyard garden" brimming with some 1,200 daffodil varieties inspired the annual Camden Festival where daffs are the star. • Brent and Becky Heath's nursery in Gloucester, Virginia, famed for heirloom daffodils, likewise inspired the Gloucester Daffodil Festival. • Fremont, North Carolina, is known as Daffodil Town. • The Lone Star State town of Round Rock calls itself the "Daffodil Capital of Texas."

SOUTHERN STORY: OLD-TIME DAFFS

In 1982, just before graduating from the University of North Carolina at Chapel Hill's library school, Serena DuBose scoured the South for potential jobs. In February, she found herself interviewing in gray, cold, and, by her account, depressed-looking Petersburg, Virginia. Trappings be damned, after the diplomas had been handed out, she took a post there as the children's librarian at the town's public library.

"Thankfully," Serena says, "spring soon exploded and graced the grand old homes. The house I had rented was an 1898 tenement two blocks from the library, and it stood on a bluff that must have been a target for Yankee guns during the Civil War siege of the city. A line of bare-boned crepe myrtles stood along one side of the house and at their feet, daffodils.

"The day I moved in, those daffodils were fully open and glorious. There were so many of them around each tree that their modest blossoms made a very brave show. Every spring I was there they continued to bloom with abandon, and when

I eventually left Petersburg, I took some with me. It was not easy. They had been planted so long before that the crepe myrtle roots tried to thwart my invasion. Still, I managed to wrest a few bulbs out, and they multiplied in their new digs as if they had never been disturbed.

"Years later," continues Serena, "I took one of my daffodil blossoms to Brent Heath at his daffodil nursery in Gloucester, Virginia, to find out what variety it was. He called it 'Sergeant Majors' and said it was an old, old variety brought from England. When I eventually left Virginia to return home to South Carolina, I brought some with me. Today, they just keep marching on and blooming.

"The tenacity of my daffodils," says Serena, who now lives in Barnwell, South Carolina, "reminds me of the Thoreau quote about lilacs surviving long after the house and barn and people are gone. I have planted them everywhere I have lived, knowing that they will trumpet their glory as long as I hope to do in heaven."

Opposite forms—like these trailing Carolina jessamine (jasmine) vines and perky narcissus—make for a great combination. To replicate, trim daffodils one to three inches taller than the vase; position the shorter ones about the lip of the vessel and the taller ones toward the center. Insert vines after placing the vase, and allow the jessamine to cascade as it does in nature (*facing*). Place bouquets in areas frequented by guests— like this powder room—where the sight and scent will be a sweet surprise. These vintage varieties radiate a decidedly old-fashioned, feminine fragrance. To build a similar arrangement, let the smaller blooms form the base of the bouquet, then tuck in larger, brightly hued varieties where a burst of color is needed (*right*).

BEHIND THE SCENES

On a sun-drenched February afternoon, Kathy Woolsey, garden curator at Cypress Gardens in Moncks Corner, South Carolina, loaded down the bed of a four-wheel ATV with water-filled buckets. Heather and I piled in for a cutting tour of the 163-acre swamp and botanical garden that first opened to the public in 1932. Back in those days, then-owner Benjamin Kittredge, Jr. had converted the one-time 1700s rice plantation into a thriving garden, rife with azaleas, camellias, cypress, and tupelo trees, the latter of which look like lanky gray legs slogging through the property's boggy swamps. With wood ducks screaming into flight and curtains of Spanish moss hanging low, it's easy to see how this woodland could spook anyone.

But thanks to Mr. Kittredge, come February the place puts on a sunny face—a decidedly cheery, buttery yellow one. That's because the man had

a passion for daffodils, and as Kathy puts it, "he ordered them by the train-car load." Upon delivery, Mr. Kittredge would fill gunny sacks with the narcissus and toss the bulbs hither and yon as he walked his property. Gardeners followed behind him to plant the daffs where they fell. And thanks to his haphazard approach, every late winter to early spring, the place is awash in a gold mine of bobbing heads—antique jonquils, daffodils, and paperwhites galore.

Because the day we gathered our bounty was a cool one, and since we were under the shade of a tall tree canopy, afternoon cutting was fine for the blooms, and they stood up well overnight in a cooler until the shoot at my own Charleston cottage the next day. Honestly, before the visit to see Kathy, who identified every last bloom here, none of us on the shoot knew there were so many varieties of narcissus.

To gather an ample collection of narcissus—here, daffodils and paperwhites both—all you need is a flower basket and a pair of sharp scissors. Don't leave the flowers out of water for too long, though, as they will wilt.

'Minnow'

'Geranium' 1930

'Avalanche' 1700s

snowflake

'White Dream' tulip

'Erlicheer' 1934

found jonquil

'Butter and Eggs' 1777

'Las Vegas'

'Ice Follies' 1953

'Aflame' 1938

'Rijnveld's Early Sensation' 1943

'found daffodil

'Ceylon'

'Topolino'

'February Gold' 1923

'Jetfire'

AZALEAS

COMMON NAME: Azalea

BOTANICAL NAME: *Rhododendron*

PLANT TYPE: Shrub (Subgenus *Pentanthera* are deciduous natives; subgenus *Titsuji* are evergreen.)

ORIGIN: Asia

FLOWER COLORS: Orange, peach, pink, red, white, and yellow (deciduous); purple, red, and white (evergreen).

IDEAL GROWING CONDITIONS: Dappled sun to partial shade (deciduous) or full shade to partial sun (evergreen); mildly acidic, loose, and moist soil

SIZE: 2 to 5 feet tall, 2 to 5 feet wide

ZONES: 1 to 10

BLOOMING TIME: Typically spring (some variet- ies also bloom in the fall)

ARRANGING TIPS: Because azalea blooms are short-lived, cut them just as they start to bloom and display them immediately.

VASE LIFE: One to two days at most

MEANINGS: Fidelity, passion, temperance, and womanly

TRIVIA: Louisiana gardener Robert Lee gets credit for being the first to hybridize Encore Azaleas®, a strain that flowers in both spring and fall and became available to the public in 1997. • Sum- merville, South Carolina, is known as Flowertown thanks to the hundreds of azaleas that bloom there each spring. • Georgia's state wildflower is the azalea. • Deer won't eat azaleas because they are toxic, but Koreans dress tiny pancakes with the blooms and even sip a *dugyeonju* ("azalea wine") brewed from the plant.

Be alert for early-blooming branches, but cut them in judicious fashion to preserve the shapes of shrubs and trees. And choose vessels substantial enough to support top-heavy arrangements. Here, large, loose boughs of 'Delaware Valley White' azaleas fill a lead crystal decanter, while redbud limbs reach out from a stout-bottomed water pitcher *(left)*. Style table bouquets low to allow easy conversation and dish passing, and choose linens that serve as a complementary backdrop for the color of your flowers *(above)*.

SOUTHERN STORY: HUMBLE BEGINNINGS

In the 1950s Oliver Washington Jr. worked at Mobile, Alabama's Brookley Air Force Base, but the father of seven had bigger ideas—even though they started off on the small side.

It began in the 1920s, when a Mobile businessman pushed the city to embrace azaleas as a tourist attraction. Residents got free potted azaleas from local gas stations every time they filled up their tanks, and pretty soon, the whole city was abloom. Over the next few decades, the most photogenic azalea-laden streets were marked with pink curbs to guide visitors along the prettiest paths through town, parades with hoop-skirted "Azalea Maids" overtook the city in the spring, and just on the outside of town, visitors flocked to Bellingrath Gardens.

A one-time fish camp, Bellingrath Gardens was the home of Walter and Bessie Bellingrath. While Walter wanted to hunt the land, Bessie preferred to garden it. She won out, and by the early 1930s, they had opened the well-groomed grounds to visitors. Pretty soon thousands followed the city's Azalea Trail right up to Bellingrath's doorstep.

The commotion caught Oliver's attention and he asked Walter and Bessie if he could sell azaleas to their visitors from the back of his pickup truck. Oliver Washington III was just a little boy back then and recalls tagging along to the impromptu flower stand. "I remember there'd be some weeks where you saw all cars from Mississippi, then the next week you'd see them from Arkansas, and the next from Louisiana," he says.

Oliver III says he and his siblings rounded up and prepped the tin cans used to pot the azaleas. They'd go around to local cafeterias and restaurants to gather empty cans; then cut the tops off and cleaned them out. "Canned tomatoes, beans, and ketchup . . . that was some work," he says in an understated rumble. They'd punch drainage holes in the bottom with a church key, then coat the insides with tar to make the cans water-resistant.

After selling thousands of the plants, Oliver Jr. opened Shore Acres Plant Farm, just down the road from Bellingrath Gardens. After earning horticulture degrees from Alabama A&M and University of Florida at Gainesville, Oliver III joined him. Now an eighteen-acre operation with twenty employees, Shore Acres still sells azaleas. And though none of Oliver III's siblings followed him into the flower business, his son, Oliver IV, joined ranks. Between the two, they've earned awards from the Alabama Nursery and Landscaping Association, a membership on Alabama A&M's Board of Trustees, a seat on Mobile's Botanical Garden Board, and many more accolades. The company is known as a bastion for African American business leadership, and they say their success comes from seven-days-a-week work, savvy practices, and not cutting corners—in other words, the basics that Oliver Jr. impressed upon them.

Set under the eaves of a 12-foot-high piazza ceiling, this bouquet of flowering quince and 'President Claeys' azalea boughs demands height and volume. When working with flowering branches, place them in your vessel first, as the delicate blooms fall off easily and because they tangle, making them tough to maneuver and manipulate *(facing)*. A milk glass vessel set atop a bistro table spills over with 'Formosa' azaleas, bridal wreath spirea, and tulip tree magnolia blooms. Break up a hot-toned bouquet with cool colors, like these calming greens and soothing whites. After inserting floral foam into the vase, azaleas were added around the base and then formed into a domed silhouette, followed by the magnolia and the bridal wreath spirea *(right)*.

BEHIND THE SCENES

In the 1830s, twenty-two-year-old John Grimké Drayton was in England studying to become a minister when he got news that his older brother had been shot at their family plantation in Charleston, South Carolina. Thus, the young reverend inherited Magnolia Plantation, an enormous spread of rice fields and formal gardens in the wild Lowcountry. He returned home years later and became sick with tuberculosis. Gardening was prescribed as treatment, and thus the man of the cloth turned to creating his own paradise. Today, he's credited with introducing a variety of Southern stalwarts to the region's—and country's—landscapes, among them the first Southern Indica hybrid (or Southern Indian hybrid) and some of America's earliest outdoor camellias.

Now azaleas overwhelm Magnolia each spring as they have since the plantation's early days, dotting the landscape like a layer of bright confetti tossed every which way by spring breezes. One April day, Director of Gardens Tom Johnson gave us the green light to wander, clippers in hand, through this colorful wonderland and thus graced us with the blooms you see here. Thanks to the hot afternoon, we nearly lost our harvest, as the petals are more delicate than tissue paper and our buckets were low on water. Next time we gather azaleas, we'll be sure to cut them the day we plan to showcase them and pamper them properly on the way to their vases. As for where they were photographed? We staged a sweet brunch in a small Charleston courtyard.

Reinterpret holiday decorations to suit your own setting. Here, two tiny moss-tinged baskets (one filled with 'Coral Bells') are a subtle tip of the hat to Easter, when azaleas are in full bloom in most of the South (facing).

'Coral Bells'

'Daphne Salmon'

'Poseaman'

'George Lindley Taber'

bridal wreath spirea

quince

'President Claeys'

ROSES

COMMON TYPES: Modern roses (climbing roses, floribundas, grandiflora, hybrid teas, miniature roses, polyanthas, shrub roses); old roses (bourbon, China, damask, Gallica, hybrid perpetuals, moss, Noisettes, teas)

GENUS NAME: *Rosa*

PLANT TYPES: Climbing vine and shrub

VARIETIES: The two main types of roses here—old, those typically identified before 1867, and modern roses, those generally cataloged thereafter—have distinct differences beyond age. Old roses tend to be pale in color with blooms that are more fragrant, fragile, and delicate than their modern counterparts, though they are hardier plants overall. Modern roses (especially non-climbers) tend to have longer stems and cut blooms last longer.

COLORS: Orange, pastels, peach, pink, purple, red, white, and yellow

ORIGIN: Asia

IDEAL GROWING CONDITIONS: Partial to full sun; other conditions vary greatly

SIZE: Varies greatly

ZONES: All

BLOOMING TIME: Spring to fall, depending on type

ARRANGING TIPS: As soon as you cut roses, plunge their stems into water, and keep them in a cool, shaded area. Change water daily to prolong vase life. The shorter and thinner the stem, the lower the overall arrangement should be.

VASE LIFE: Old, a few days; modern, up to ten days

MEANINGS: Admiration, enthusiasm (orange); friendship, freedom (yellow); love (red); purity, innocence (white); and success (peach)

TRIVIA: The Cherokee rose (*Rosa laevigata*) is Georgia's state flower. • Tyler, Texas, is known as the Rose Capital of America, as nearly 50 percent of commercial roses in the United States come from that area. The town's annual rose festival, first held in 1933, attracts some 100,000 visitors each October. • Rose hips (the round fruit yielded by a rose flower) have long been used to brew tea and wine and to make jelly.

To make this window box-style metal vessel serviceable, it was lined with a plastic container, then filled with saturated floral foam. All the flowers are remnants from other bouquets and range from 'Blush Noisette', 'Elie Beauvillain', 'Manchester Guardian Angel', 'Maréchal Niel', 'Mrs. Dudley Cross', 'Natchitoches Noisette', 'Perle d'Or', and 'Reve d'Or' to 'Safrano'. Potted blooms (like miniature roses) could be inserted into such a vessel for a quick arrangement, but this grab-bag look is part of the bouquet's appeal *(left)*. Vary shape and texture in a bouquet, but find a common ground (like the peach and pink tones seen here) to unite the elements *(right, above and below)*.

SOUTHERN STORY: SWEETHEARTS

In the midst of World War II, Helen Brammer and Robert "Archie" Hulsey were sent to Naples, Italy—she as an army nurse, he as part of the Inspector General Corps. Their first date was to see *Carmen* at the Royal Palace in nearby Caserta, and from there, the couple's romance escalated.

Given their pasts—he, 46, had been through one marriage, and she, a then-late-in-life 38, had never walked the aisle—and the dire backdrop of the time and place, neither took their feelings for the other for granted. So as soon as the two were shipped home after the war, they married. Helen's father, a Lutheran minister, presided over the small service at the little parish church in her hometown of St. Ansgar, Iowa. For her bouquet, Helen gathered a bunch of pale pink 'Sweetheart Roses' from an abundant bush that grew on the church grounds. And when the couple took the train to Archie's farm in East Texas, Helen took the delicately wrapped bouquet with her.

As the newlyweds settled in, Helen nursed her cuttings into two baby rosebushes. Years passed and the couple moved to Palestine, Texas, and, of course, the toddler roses followed. As time rolled on, the bushes grew into towering things, says Helen and Archie's grandson Ed Johnson, and "Mammaw" would give copious bouquets to neighbors, friends, and family. "Those flow-

ers were amazing," says Ed. "It seemed like they were always blooming, and the plants never got black spots like most rosebushes do—they were just little tanks. Since we had no air conditioning back then, summers were spent on the screened porch. There was nothing like sitting out there smelling them."

In their later years, Helen and Archie marched on like tanks themselves. They kept a regular Friday night date at the Dairy Queen near their home, and whenever Archie stretched his legs for even the shortest of walks, he would be sure to pass by the local florist to bring home a carnation for his girl. Archie died in 1980, and when grandchildren would visit Helen in her later years, she'd ask them to drive her to her husband's grave, where she'd leave a bundle of homegrown roses for him. "My grandfather was her heart," says Ed.

By her nineties, no longer able to keep up with the house and garden, Helen elected to move into a nursing home. Her family had to sell the old place, but before all was said and done, Ed visited to get his own cuttings of Mammaw and Pappaw's rosebush. He wasn't the only one; Ed's relatives followed suit, and today, the robust flowers continue to bloom across the South. "Every time the wind blows and carries their scent," says Ed, "I remember the two of them."

Choosing a vessel like this weathered cast-iron garden urn serves two purposes: first, it is weighty enough to support the ample, top-heavy bouquet; and second, its patina contrasts nicely with the tender elegance of the roses, which were salvaged from a local rose show. Placing the arrangement in an out-of-reach spot further ensures the bouquet is less likely to topple. Tip: add loquat branches first, before the roses (facing). If you are able to cut long-stemmed roses, don't trim them down when first displaying the blooms. Rather, start long (like those in this porcelain pitcher stocked with 'General Lamarque', 'Haynesville Pink Cluster', and old-fashioned sweet peas) and shorten the stems as the days pass and the flowers age (right).

BEHIND THE
SCENES

Sometimes it takes a village to create a chapter. Such was the case with this one, as we didn't want to decimate any rose garden for the sake of these pages. Thus, Heather and I divided and conquered Charleston's bounty. I tagged along behind the South's preeminent rose expert, Ruth Knopf, who just so happens to live not twenty minutes away from me on Sullivan's Island, South Carolina, in her aptly named Rose Cottage.

Long sought after for her extensive knowledge of antique roses, Mrs. Knopf was the brainchild behind the gorgeous antique rose gardens at Boone Hall Plantation in nearby Mount Pleasant. In 1998 she designed the famous beds that flank the entrance to the Colonial Revival house there, and on a sunny day in May, she schooled me on garden upkeep while prudently cutting samples from the vines and bushes. Buckets in tow, pad in my back pocket, I could barely keep up with the grand dame on any level. But it was a delight trying, and the rewards . . . well, you can see they were worth it.

Downtown in Charleston proper, Heather racked up her own adventures in the stunning twentieth-century urban oasis known as Hampton Park. An Olmsted-sculpted remnant of the

1901 South Carolina Interstate and West Indian Exposition, the park traded its exhibit "palaces" for garden beds brimming with rare native and antique flora more than seventy-five years ago. More recently, the tag team of JoAnn Breland (the city's superintendent of horticulture) and her right-hand assistant Joan MacDonald, donated scores from their extensive collection of Noisette roses and more.

To fill out the heirloom blooms, we called upon Jane Waring (Mrs. Knopf's dear friend and another true rosarian), whose private garden charms in the most unpretentious, ambling way. And we visited her daughter Laura's jewel box garden as well. Finally, Kathy Woolsey from Cypress Gardens in Moncks Corner, South Carolina, gave us leftovers from a Charleston Lowcountry Rose Society regional show. For the latter, I drove to North Charleston to wade through the glorious homegrown castaways that didn't make it to the judging tables. All in all, the generosity and care each of these gardeners—Ruth, JoAnn, Joan, Jane, Laura, and Kathy's crew—had imparted upon the flowers floored me as much as the flowers themselves. As for our harvest? We were spoiled rotten.

This seemingly formal collection of blooms actually mixes low-brow blooms (like the common tropical bush pineapple guava) with high-brow varieties (like hybrid tea roses, the frilly 1909 'Excellenz von Schubert', and 'Fellenburg' Noisette).

'The Fairy' 1932

'Puerto Rico'

'Buff Beauty' 1939

'Marie van Houtte' 1871

'Madame Antoine Mari' 1901

'Crepuscule' 1904

found rose

'Slater's Crimson China' 1790

'Cramoisi Superior' 1832

'Altissimo' 1966

'Chestnut Rose' 1814

found rose

HYDRANGEAS

COMMON NAMES AND TYPES: 'Annabelle', lacecap, mophead, oakleaf, and peegee

BOTANICAL NAMES: *Hydrangea arborescens, H. macrophylla, H. macrophylla normalis, H. paniculata, H. quercifolia*

PLANT TYPE: Shrub (One strain is a climbing vine.)

COLORS: Blue, green, pink, purple, and white

ORIGINS: East Asia and North and South America

IDEAL GROWING CONDITIONS: Full morning sun or partial shade; well-drained, moist soil

SIZE: 3 to 8 feet tall, up to 6 feet wide

ZONES: 3 to 9

BLOOMING TIME: Late spring to early autumn

ARRANGING TIPS: Cut mopheads after they have bloomed fully, while the petals are slightly tough and strong. Mash or split the ends of the woody stem to allow for better water absorption.

VASE LIFE: 4 days to one week (thereafter they can begin to dry)

MEANINGS: Earnestness and understanding

TRIVIA: On July 4, 1775, in central Georgia, famed botanist William Bartram was the first to catalog America's oakleaf hydrangea. • Hydrangeas thrive in every part of Alabama, where it is the official state wildflower. • Soil pH affects mophead color—decrease it and you get blue flowers; increase it and you get pink blooms.

SOUTHERN STORY: HYDRANGEA HEAVEN

Penny McHenry lived large. Take her backyard garden in Atlanta, for instance. A few decades ago, aside from a pair of hydrangea bushes that had been gifted to her upon the death of one of her daughters, she felt the place looked pretty forlorn. But the way those two blue mopheads uplifted the entire expanse gave Penny an idea: she decided to spread their joy.

To do so, she'd take hold of one of the long, lower limbs, dig a small trench below it, strip a bit of its bark away and then bury the branch so the leafy portion was free to welcome the sun. She filled the trench with soil and then weighted the buried section in place with a brick. With some green-thumb TLC, in time, a new shrub grew next to its parent bush. And over the years, Penny's garden transformed into what she called Hydrangea Heaven. With its four hundred hydrangea bushes, the aptly named garden was a true spectacle, one that spilled over into the church lot next door.

Penny, a flamboyant woman who was once a stage actress, would hold court in her Heaven, wearing her signature sunglasses and with her white hair swept up into a bun. How did her hydrangeas thrive so? She kissed them, she'd say. What was she doing out there in the garden? Making babies, she'd say. Could you take a peek at her "children"

that afternoon? Oh, no, she'd say, they need their beauty rest. Mornings are best for the girls.

As eccentric a character as Penny was, her passion for hydrangeas spanned beyond her backyard theater, and her knowledge far exceeded that of the average lay gardener. She became a sought-after lecturer and schooled many garden enthusiasts in how to care for, propagate, and dry hydrangeas as she entertained them with her poetry on the matter.

In 1994, she founded the American Hydrangea Society, and in 2006, the Atlanta Botanical garden named its hydrangea collection in her honor. The 'Penny Mac' hydrangea was named for her, and another variety, the 'Mini Penny,' was developed as a tribute. Given the woman's prowess and personality, it's little surprise that when *Southern Living* ran photos of "The Hydrangea Queen's" garden on its March 1992 cover, it became the all-time best-selling issue of the iconic regional magazine.

Though Penny passed away in 2006, her followers still celebrate the flowering shrub that gave her so much happiness: each June, just west of Atlanta, the Penny McHenry Hydrangea Festival draws thousands of visitors. And with her babies in the starring role and her name on the marquee, you can bet Penny's smiling down on it all.

'Ayesha', with its tiny cupped petals, is so singular that a few simply placed blooms in a vase fill a room with sassy style. Make dark flowers pop by placing them in bright-colored containers *(left)*. The full, round form of mophead hydrangeas lend themselves well to bowl-shaped vessels, like this one filled with 'Dooley', 'Endless Summer®', and still-green 'Forever & Ever Double Pink®' blooms, which were inserted into floral foam *(facing)*.

BEHIND THE SCENES

Beg, borrow, steal. Heather and I had to get creative about the gardens we hit up for fodder. Charleston, South Carolina, may be excessively verdant, but it's a small town and we didn't want to wear out our welcome with the green-thumbed populace. So here's a confession: while the bulk of these blooms did come to us by way of a perfectly legal morning cutting session in June at the city's prolific Hampton Park (under the tutelage of the ever-patient and knowledgeable Joan MacDonald), I did heist a few flowers for the sake of filling things out.

You see, on my morning dog walks, I pass a fair share of houses that are falling in on themselves, long-faded and abandoned beauties that are still dressed in floral finery. Snowflakes, spiderwort, irises, and, yes, hydrangeas all still call these places home, though no human soul has for generations.

So as Heather walked the park trails with Joan, I slipped from one deserted lot to another with my mutt's leash in one hand, clippers and flower bucket in the other. I only cut from shrubs on the private sides of these homes and tried my darndest to spare as many mopheads as I lopped off. So beg? Yep, we begged from Hampton Park. Borrow? Yep, we borrowed from one willing neighbor. And steal? I suppose you could call what I did to those old homes just that. But as for regrets? I have not a one. You know what they say about desperate times. . . . .

To showcase the harvest, we headed to local interior designer Jenny Miller's brick Georgian home in the well-heeled South of Broad area of downtown Charleston, where the cheery light-filled space suited the joyful blooms in singular fashion.

A trip to the farmers market yields a wealth of mopheads, bishop's weed, summer phlox, and wax flower. To create this look in a more permanent fashion, fill a watertight container with cool water, plop in the blooms in an informal manner, then place the container in the basket.

Compact hydrangea shrubs—like this 'Forever & Ever Double Pink®' and a small 'Nikko Blue'—are little bouquets in their own right. Plant them in containers and move the vessels where you want to add a burst of color, be that outdoors or inside for special events *(facing)*. A little florist wire and a plastic liner transformed this whitewashed bucket into a hanging flower basket *(right)*.

To give any setting depth, pair dissimilar textures and shapes; here, a rough-hewn, undulating vessel fashioned from clay provides a terrific contrast to the slick glass tabletop and the room's clean architectural lines. The lush mass of lacecaps and 'Nikko Blue' mopheads echoes the light, airy nature of the whitewashed sunroom that opens onto a garden *(left)*. Tall ceilings, a significantly large piece of artwork, and a substantial piece of furniture form a backdrop that begs for a large, bold bouquet like this unfettered collection of oakleaf hydrangea, 'Little Gem' magnolia, and sword fern fronds nestled into a garden urn *(above)*.

white lacecap

'Shirofuji' lacecap

'Nikko Blue' mophead

bishop's weed

summer phlox

sword fern

'Little Gem' magnolia

'Veitchii' lacecap

'Forever & Ever Double Pink®' mophead

oakleaf hydrangea

'Dooley' mophead

'Ayesha' mophead

'Fuji Waterfall' mophead

ZINNIAS

COMMON NAMES: Old-fashioned, old maid, and zinnia

BOTANICAL NAME: *Zinnia elegans* (most common)

PLANT TYPE: Annual

COLORS: Green, fuchsia, multicolored, orange, purple, red, white, and yellow

ORIGINS: Mexico and South America

IDEAL GROWING CONDITIONS: From seed; full-sun; well-drained soil. Avoid organic mulch and over-watering, as both contribute to mildew and stem rot.

SIZE: 6 inches to 3 feet tall

ZONES: All

BLOOMING TIME: Summer through fall

ARRANGING TIP: Remove lower leaves before using in bouquets to extend the life of the blooms and to avoid bacteria in the water.

VASE LIFE: Five days to one week

MEANING: Friendship

TRIVIA: Originally from Mexico and South America, zinnias are named after eighteenth-century German botanist Johann Gottfried Zinn, who's credited as the first Western scientist to record them.

Old milk bottles dotted with 'Lilliput', 'Profusion', and 'State Fair' zinnias along with a little red gomphrena wake up an all-white bath. Find great vessels like these at flea markets and yard sales (facing). When dressing a party table, be on the lookout for flowering herbs to add great color and wonderful scents to a bouquet. Here, jelly jars stuffed with basil, 'Lilliput', 'Pixie Sunshine', and 'Profusion' zinnias in pink and white turn an afternoon party festive (right).

SOUTHERN STORY: SEEDLINGS

Sometimes it takes a lifetime to circle back to one's childhood. It's been that way for Baltimore, Maryland native Barbara Plantholt Melera. After a successful career as a venture capitalist, she swapped her corporate togs for gardening clogs, and now—along with her husband, Peter—the mother of two runs the nation's oldest seed purveyor, D. Landreth Seed Company, founded in 1784. Among the hundreds of seed types the 200-plus-year-old company carries, Landreth offers more than thirty varieties of zinnias, partly because it was that humble plant that sparked her passion for flowers.

"When I was five years old, my mom gave me a bunch of zinnia seeds and told me to find something to plant them in," says Barbara. "We lived in a row home in Baltimore with a small, narrow backyard, so I found an old shoebox and filled it with soil. I put the box right under the hose spigot so I could easily water my garden. Then I sprinkled those seeds all over the earth and covered them with more dirt. In just a few

days, I had a shoebox filled to overflowing with hundreds of tiny green seedlings.

"Fifty years later," Barbara continues, "I can still remember the combination of awe, excitement, and joy that I felt watching those seedlings come out of the soil and grow. It was wonderful. And when they were about a week old, my dad offered to help me transplant them. As he picked up the soaked shoebox, it collapsed, and while many of the seedlings were lost, many survived. Together, we planted them in the yard, and throughout that summer, we picked and picked and picked zinnias. For months, there was a glass full of fresh flowers in our kitchen window.

"Today," says Barbara, "I have a huge soft spot in my heart for all zinnias. That very first experience taught me how abundant life is, how fragile it is, and how incredible it is to watch it unfold. From that first, sweet, simple experience came a lifelong love of gardening and a respect for that most precious of gifts—life itself."

Anchor a whimsical bouquet of quirky flowers (like this concoction of fuchsia, gomphrena and 'Whirligig' zinnias) with a vessel that has straight, clean lines (*left*). If you stay within the same color family, vary the size and shape of flower heads and stem lengths for textural depth. A bouquet need not be dense to appear full, especially when the colors are as strong as these (*facing*).

BEHIND THE SCENES

Planning photo shoots to coincide with bloom times is an inexact science. Photographer Peter Frank Edwards' backyard garden yielded more weeds than zinnias by the time we were ready for the cheery things. And the ones we had arranged to be grown especially for us? They were only seedlings come shooting time. So Heather and I yanked on our boots and garden clogs and hightailed it out to Wadmalaw Island, South Carolina, where Shawn Thackeray of Thackeray Farms raises vegetables and greens alongside the prettiest fields of flowers you'll ever see.

I first saw Shawn's blooms when a sweetheart left a Mason jar full of them on my headboard one morning after the fellow made an early, clandestine run to Charleston's Saturday Farmers Market. The bundle of sweet peas, zinnias, and celosia undid me, as did the simple vessel Shawn sold them in. So the day before our July shoot at Fred and Judy Reinhard's all-white Sullivan's Island beach cottage, lucky Heather and I got to cut our way through Shawn's bountiful zinnia rows. The funny thing was that as we snipped and chatted, he and his fellow farmers were gathering under what Shawn's kids called the gypsy tree. Apparently, every Wednesday evening, as the summer light stretches later on into the night, the fellows convene to cook whatever's ripe that week and chefs from the finest restaurants in Charleston join them. As we cut flowers and they cut late-season tomatoes, we all reveled in the bounty Wadmalaw Island's fertile soil had gifted us.

With their long stalks, vivid colors, and compact heads, zinnias are dream flowers for simple bouquets. Just collect a rainbow and place them sparingly in containers (you can see the blooms better when you vary the height and split a dense harvest into multiple containers).

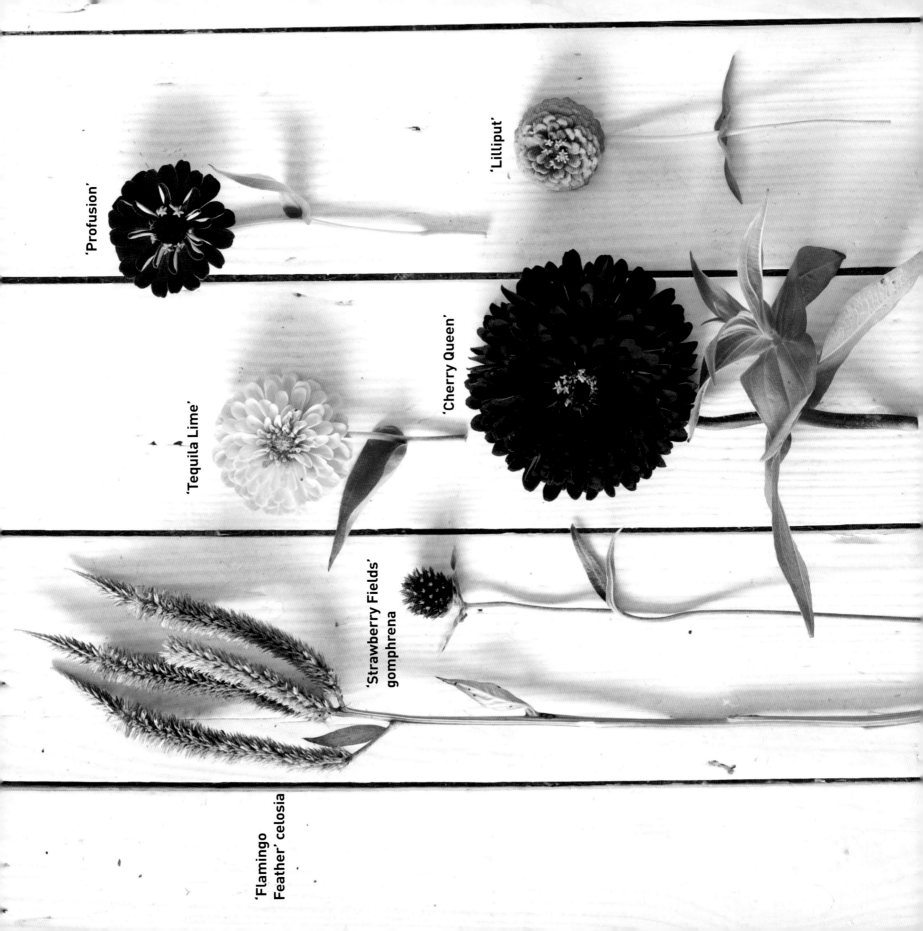

'Profusion'

'Lilliput'

'Tequila Lime'

'Cherry Queen'

'Strawberry Fields'
gomphrena

'Flamingo
Feather' celosia

'Magellan
Coral'

'Thumbelina'

'Profusion'

'Whirligig'

'Sonata Carmine'
cosmos

Dahlia pinnata

SUNFLOWERS

COMMON NAME: Common sunflower

BOTANICAL NAME: *Helianthus annuus*

PLANT TYPE: Annual

COLORS: Orange, red, rust, white, and various yellows

ORIGINS: North and South America

IDEAL GROWING CONDITIONS: From seed; full sun; moist, well-drained soil

SIZE: 3 to 15 feet tall, flower heads range from just inches to 2 feet wide

ZONES: 1 to 12

BLOOMING TIME: Summer to fall

ARRANGING TIPS: Cut base of sunflowers on an angle so they can absorb water easily. Longer stems, larger heads, and numerous blooms on a single stem drink a lot of water—monitor levels to keep the plant hydrated. Cool, shady spots help perkiness.

VASE LIFE: five days to one week

MEANINGS: adoration and longevity

TRIVIA: Texas leads the South in sunflower farming: in 2007, 40,000 acres of the plant were harvested. • Scientifically speaking, sunflowers track the sun—turning their faces to its rays—thanks to a growth hormone that causes the shaded side of the plant's stem to grow, thus forcing the flower head to droop in the direction of light.

Like colors, like textures, and like shapes of different scales make this pairing of 'Santa Fe' sunflowers and safflowers well balanced *(facing)*. As summer transitions to fall, look for leaves and grasses to add to bouquets. Here, a pitcher of 'Autumn Beauty' and 'Velvet Queen' sunflowers punctuated with stalks of millet and fall leaves soften the rustic look of this old barn *(right)*.

SOUTHERN STORY: SUNFLOWER KING

Anybody would get worn out mowing a 20-acre lawn. And that's exactly what started Gordon Boogaert on the path to becoming Gilliam, Louisiana's so-called "Sunflower King." Back in 1995, Gordon bought a solitary house on a large tract of land in the rural northwestern corner of Louisiana, and being a corn and cotton farmer, he quickly thought of what he could plant to get himself out of the lawn-mowing seat. Wheat was OK one year and brown millet wasn't bad the next—except the latter was so popular with the birds, he says, the paint job on his barns suffered in their wake. Needless to say, that was the end of millet and the beginning of sunflowers.

A few weeks after planting what the neighbors assumed were cockleburs, the seemingly gangly field bloomed, and 20 acres in the middle of farm country were ablaze with sunny faces bobbing in the summer heat. "There was nothing like it that first year," says Gordon. First, artists showed up to take in the spectacle, then photographers. Then he had camera trucks from "every news station within a three-state area," he says. "I watched the first show on TV in my living room, and I have to say, I got a little scared, thinking I might have messed up because the cars started rolling in almost before I turned the set off."

The cars kept coming—fifty-plus a day for as long as the sunflowers bloomed. "But," says Gordon, "nothing bad ever happened. I guess you just don't really have any bad cats coming out to see sunflowers. And in all the years I've done it since, there's not been even one bit of trash. It's been nothing but a very, very good experience."

Still, visitors do get into trouble every now and again. "This year it rained after the flowers bloomed, and I kept having to go out with my tractor and haul all these Cadillacs out of the mud," Gordon says, chuckling. "The ladies said they just had to see the flowers and were apologizing right and left."

Based on Gordon's initial draw, just over a decade ago, Gilliam (which is slightly northwest of Shreveport) started a Sunflower Festival and Trail. And today, he donates seeds to other area residents and farmers who have lined the highway to his home with their own sunflower patches. Visitors to the festival can get sunflower seeds at the local museum, too.

As for Gordon, he loves all the action. Besides the initial newscasts and annual coverage, HGTV did a thirty-minute spot on his endeavors, and a children's book on sunflowers for *National Geographic* was based on his cheery field. But each summer, as he plants the fields and eventually cordons off an area on the back for folks to pick their own freebies, it's his visitors that get him most fired up. "You'd be amazed at how many people—quality people—are attracted to enjoying something so simple," Gordon says.

Turning an old washtub upside down gave this pitcher of sunflowers a pedestal upon which to better showcase the blooms. Because they are so stout and hardy, sunflower stalks can stand tall like these, but if you need to cheat height, place a shelf (upturned plastic food containers work well) in your vessel, then build your bouquet and add water *(left)*. Anything that blooms at the same time is fair game for blending in bouquets, like this assemblage of late-season 'Profusion' zinnias, nearly dried 'Moonshine' yarrow, chasmanthium, and common found sunflowers *(facing)*.

BEHIND THE SCENES

Dodging hurricanes wasn't something we considered when we embarked on this book, but so it goes when you live in the coastal South and want to showcase local blooms. Thanks to two storms bearing down on us in September, we changed our shoot date and rushed to gather flowers before the winds and rain devoured them.

One deceptively glorious afternoon, Heather and I bolted out to Thackeray Farms on Wadmalaw Island, South Carolina, to cut the prickly, sticky sunflowers Shawn Thackeray had been nursing along for us. From there, we headed over to Rosebank Farms, just next to Kiawah Island, to collect whatever other Indian summer blooms might still stand in the fields. From sunflowers to black-eyed Susans, we found a bounty.

Rosebank, owned by Louise Bennett and Sidi Limehouse, has been a roadside icon since the 1980s. At the heart of the place is a massive open-air stand with everything from fresh produce to cut flowers and preserves. Behind it is a petting zoo (populated with enormous pot-bellied pigs, a

dwarf Brahman cow, goats, rabbits, chickens, and more), and behind that stands a one-room schoolhouse that once served the islanders. Behind the schoolhouse? There, several acres of flowers and vegetables spread out into the horizon.

Heather and I wandered into those flower fields to gather the last bundles of dry rustling strawflowers, scraggly-legged sunflowers, towering okra pods, fresh-faced daisies, and on. We even pulled on boots and waded in the ditches, where we snagged cattails, papyrus and some charming weed that looked like fuzzy green wheat. When we hauled the lot of it to Mount Pleasant and set up shots in Linda Page's Thieves Market (a charming dusty red barn filled to the rafters with antiques), the flowers looked like they were just born to be in the colorful, quirky country spot.

And as for those storms? Thankfully they mellowed by the time they hit and merely soaked our little corner of the world to the bone. And as for the flower fields? They, of course, drank the rain up.

'Sunbeam'

black-eyed Susan

'Sante Fe'

'Velvet Queen'

safflower

Johnsongrass

brown-eyed
Susan

found sunflower

found sunflower

'Autumn Beauty'

immature sorghum

GREENS

COMMON NAMES: Cedar, cypress, Dusty Miller, elaeagnus, fatsia, holly, juniper, magnolia, palmetto, papyrus, pine, and more

PLANT TYPE: Evergreen perennials (generally)

COLORS: Shades of green ranging from chartreuse to emerald to silver

ARRANGING TIPS: Mash or slit the ends of woody stems so they can better absorb water. If you place branches or stems in floral foam, be sure to keep it hydrated; if they are in a vessel, maintain the water level. Bottom-heavy vessels are best for long and/or large limbs.

VASE LIFE: Up to two weeks, depending on green

MEANINGS: abundance, good health, hope, and life

TRIVIA: In 1836, when Alabama became the first state to recognize Christmas as an official holiday (followed by Arkansas and Louisiana in 1838), it led the way to December 25 becoming a national holiday in 1870. • German immigrants in the Northeast began America's tradition of decorating Christmas trees. • German political refugee and Williamsburg, Virginia, minister Charles Minnigerode is credited with bringing the practice to the South. His gilded nut ornaments, popcorn garlands, and candlelit tree were the hit of the local Christmas season in 1842.

Give a casual family room a sophisticated touch with a bouquet of greens like this one of eucalyptus, juniper, pineapple guava, and variegated pittosporum *(left)*. When using spiked greens, like these saw palmettos in the foreground, trim and arrange with gloves, cut the stalks down with a hefty lobber, and then tuck them securely into damp floral foam. As for the mantel, be sure candlelight is used judiciously when decorating with pine; here low tea light flames are shielded by glass votives *(facing)*.

SOUTHERN STORY: MISTLETOE AND MORE

To most folks, 120 years is a long time to keep a family Christmas tradition going. But in Natchez, Mississippi, where there are likely more private historic plantations per square inch than anywhere else in the South, long-standing traditions are about as common as breathing in magnolia-scented air. Take the Smiths, for example. As far back as Pamela Smith Harriss can remember—and even farther still—her clan has gathered to decorate with fresh greens for Christmas Eve.

When Pamela was a child, they convened at Glen Mary Plantation, a massive spread of farmland, orchards, woods, and cow pastures that her great-grandmother Annie Smith bought for fifty cents an acre in the 1920s. After bundling up, the men would head out across the fields to hunt the year's holiday tree and boughs for garlands. Along the way, one of the fellows would use his 12-gauge to shoot down the thick clumps of mistletoe that grew high in the live oak canopies. Treasures in tow, they would stomp back to the 1850s-era manse, where the women had been concocting

Annie's treasured (and potent) eggnog.

"There was this aura about Grandmother's eggnog," says Pamela. "My aunts hand-whipped the egg whites till they were stiff and peaked; they would grind the nutmeg themselves; and they added two kinds of liquor. We'd pour it out into mint julep cups and sip it while we made the garlands and put up the mistletoe."

As for that mistletoe, Annie gathered a few of the choicest sprigs and bound them together with red ribbon. She placed the spray right over the front door (which meant anyone coming or going had to walk under it) so she could make a fuss over everyone who visited, says Pamela.

These days, the Smith crew still convenes on December 24, and Pamela, who grew up to be a gifted floral designer (dressing such historic sites as Monmouth Plantation and grand affairs as the Natchez King and Queen's Ball), plays hostess from time to time. Though she admits a few faux greens might mingle with the fresh ones, the eggnog is still fashioned from Annie's recipe and mistletoe still hangs over the front door.

In place of a table runner and formal centerpiece, freely placed magnolia leaves run down the length of this table; gold ornaments and silver vessels filled with clove-studded tangelos and small wisps of Australian pine provide more than enough formality for the coming repast *(left)*. Use a sprig of fresh evergreen to accent a place setting *(above right)*. An old brown tincture bottle-turned-vase hosts Chinese tallow (popcorn tree) and variegated pittosporum to add a little life to an evening's wining and dining *(below right)*.

BEHIND THE SCENES

A while back, I was camping with a guide in the Okefenokee Swamp, and he told me about surviving in that wild expanse where, in his words, everything bites: "I don't mess with it, and it don't mess with me," he said. When I ended up face-to-face with a wall of holly bushes for this chapter and was worse for the wear after the run-in, I remembered his edict acutely. Gathering the holly, plus juniper, cedar, pine, and thorny elaeagnus left me looking like I'd been wrestling cats.

It's something Southern floral design luminary Ralph Null talked about when I asked for his memories of decorating with greens for the holidays. "We'd always go to my uncle's," said the Mississippian, "and that China Fir he had was nasty stuff; it absolutely ate you up." So why do we go to the trouble to harvest such hostile plants? Maybe it's because when the skies go winter gray, when flower petals fade to wispy memories, and when leafy canopies give way to bare, skeletal limbs, any burst of green makes us feel a little more evergreen.

Thus, I know where I can find my wall of holly (in a neutral no-man's-land a few blocks from home); juniper (in a ditch on the backside of a local high-rise); cedar boughs (can't tell); pine branches (let's just say they're a bike ride away); and elaeagnus (in the shadow of a rental mansion). As for the more tropical greens Heather and I picked up—papyrus, fatsia, palmetto fronds—those were backyard gifts from our own houses, and from Michael and Alison Brewer, who lent us their 1926 Craftsman bungalow in downtown Charleston for shoot day.

The design duo couple specializes in neutral palette interiors, and their garden—a Sheila Wertimer creation—is a study in tone-on-tone green, so the place was the perfect backdrop for the simple, sophisticated and earthy look that decorating with evergreens always imparts. By the last bouquet, Heather and I were properly smitten with what we'd showcased that day, and I had forgotten—okay, *nearly forgotten*—the bite of the branches in lieu of their beauty.

To create a basic magnolia wreath, take a handful of leaves gathered at the stems; fan them over a damp floral foam ring; and then fasten in place with a florist pin. Repeat—placing the next bundle of leaves over the last pinning's stems—until the form is completely covered. Here, layers of magnolia leaves, nandina, and pittosporum hide a moistened wreath base, while Seckel pears (attached with florist picks) and pinecones add color and texture.

wax myrtle

pinecones

eucalyptus

juniper

holly

loblolly pine

Australian pine

Chinese tallow (or popcorn tree)

variegated pittosporum

papyrus

magnolia

ARRANGING

Heather Barrie—the floral guru behind the bouquets on these pages—runs Gathering: Floral + Event Design in Charleston, South Carolina, and is known nationally for natural arrangements and arrangements that have a deceptively simple, organic yet elegant style. A self-taught designer who learned the art of arranging by "playing" with the flowers that grew in the woods surrounding her suburban Atlanta home, Heather says her sensibility comes straight from her past—and present—stomping grounds. Call her on her cell phone these days, and she's as likely to answer while wading through a field of wildflowers as she is to pick up while deep in the woods collecting magnolia limbs. With a mind to re-creating some of the bouquets in the preceding chapters, here's what Heather advises when it comes to gathering and assembling local flora.

GATHERING

Whether you're roving far and wide or looking to your own backyard for plants and flowers, Heather suggests you have the following handy:

- boots
- gloves
- clippers for flowers and greens
- a lopper for woody limbs
- a spade
- buckets (with water for the blooms)
- bug spray

As for what to cut? Choose what's in season, what's in bloom, what's changing color, what's sprouting berries—these are the things that

catch Heather's eye. "Anything you wouldn't necessarily spot in a florist cooler," she says, "are the things that interest me." She goes for a variety of textures (prickly, fuzzy, slick), shapes (rounded, oval, or pointed leaves, for instance), elements (leaves, grasses, branches, vines) and colors (preferring tone-on-tone) until she's got all the puzzle pieces for an interesting bouquet. In the end, there's a fair dose of Zen in her approach. By working with what's thriving when she cuts rather than heading out with an agenda, Heather is more likely to be in the moment as she hunts for treasures and is thus more likely to cherish her finds as something nature intended just for her, just then.

Gathering tools like clippers, floral scissors, gloves, loppers, shears, buckets and more make harvesting blooms a breeze. Rubber boots can be the difference between a glorious gathering experience and a miserable one. Find them for less than $20 at discount chain stores.

CUTTING

Morning, Heather and other experts agree, is the ideal time for cutting, though early evening is a distant runner-up if you're in a pinch. At the beginning of the day, plants are "less stressed," says Heather, since they've had the night to rest. When you cut, no matter if it's a shrub, tree, or flower stem, cut just above the next joint or new growth spot so any budding portions can continue to thrive—roses should be lopped off above new buds or clusters of five leaves. And, advises Heather, never, never, never hack your way through a garden; in the best cases, "gathering" should be a service akin to pruning. After harvesting, plunge cuttings into water and transport them to a shady, cool spot as soon as possible. Some flowers excel in coolers or refrigerators (hydrangeas, for example) but the stored shelf life of cut plants varies greatly, even when blooms come off the same bush. Thus, you've got to play a little game of risk to learn their longevity. In all cases, though, one things for certain: if you refrigerate flowers at home, keep blooms away from fruit and vegetables, as they expedite floral wilting with the gases they give off. Ideally, go from gathering to display vase within hours.

To find cut-flower farms, roadside flower stands, or farmers markets that sell locally grown blooms like these dahlias, contact your local agriculture extension agent. You can also visit these websites for listings: www.localharvest.org and www.pickyourown.org.

PREPARING

"There's a whole lot of folklore out there about how to prepare plants for styling," says Heather, who operates with a no-nonsense approach. "I don't cut them under running water, and I don't singe the tips of flowers such as poppies or daffodils. Instead, I simply take a stem from my gathering bucket, cut it about an inch up on a diagonal and then place it in a clean vase with clean, lukewarm water. If I don't have a commercial preservative, I'll add a couple of drops of bleach to the water. After I've finished arranging the flowers, if I'm

being good, I'll trim them and change the water daily. When I'm not being so good, I do it every other day." Heather's dream team of styling tools includes:

- bleach or a clear liquid floral preservative
- clean vessels
- clean, lukewarm tap water
- floral foam, tape, and wire
- plastic vessel liner (if needed)
- scissors

The ideal arranging arsenal includes floral foam, scissors, tape and wire, plus a knife and liners. Frogs—heavy spiked weights that sit at the bottom of a vase to fix flower stems—like the brass one here can also be a handy tool.

VESSELS

If you've already gathered your flowers and greens, let them lead you to the right container and showcase spot. For example, a handful of short-stemmed, laid-back zinnias might just beg for a Mason jar and a kitchen windowsill. On the other hand, you might want to decorate a specific mix of spaces: something for the entry, something for the mantel, something for the dining table, something for the powder room. In those cases, Heather says, let the location dictate the bouquet. "If you're doing something for a dining table," she says, "the vessel and arrangement need to be low enough for people to see over, but if you have an entry table in a hallway with a large mirror behind it, it's better to have a tall bouquet."

When it comes to matching containers with bouquets, almost anything goes. Yes, ensure that

the materials work together visually, that the colors don't clash and that the flowers—not the vessel—are the star, but beyond those guidelines, have fun. Here is a list of handy containers:

- adapted vessels (gourds, metal tubs, wooden boxes)
- baskets (metal and wicker)
- bud vases
- vases (in a variety of scales, shapes and materials with a range of mouths)
- cups and glasses (bistro glasses, kitchen glasses, cut crystal, mint julep cups, mugs)
- repurposed containers (jelly jars, milk bottles, tin cans)
- serving vessels (bowls, creamers, gravy boats, pitchers, sugar jars)

Build a collection of vessels by exploring local flea markets, yard sales, thrift stores, and estate sales. Be sure to test that a container is watertight before you purchase it (if possible) or before you fashion a bouquet in it. If it leaks, use a plastic liner or floral foam.

ARRANGING TIPS

Typically, when Heather creates a bouquet, she works her way around a vessel, placing the larger stems around the inside edge to fashion a natural grid that can support and anchor more delicate stems. In some cases, floral foam is needed because the stems are short or the vessel shape is too odd to hold a liner. When that happens, she soaks a foam block in water till it's saturated, cuts the brick to suit the vessel's cavity, and then "plants" stems in the hydrated foam. On average, arrangements anchored in foam last only a day or two, depending on the hardiness of the blooms, but you can try to extend the life of such bouquets by watering the foam.

Once Heather's base grid—the one she's created like a lattice around the inside of the vessel—is in place, she works her way around again, this time placing showpiece blooms in key spots. Once the arrangement has taken shape, she fills

in blank areas with greens and non-headlining flowers. Always, she's varying textures, silhouettes, shapes, and shades of color. And as for volume, it depends on where the bouquet will eventually go and what is proportional to the vessel. As for density and style, formal, showy bouquets are generally more tightly packed, and natural, organic looks are a bit more airy, a little less symmetrical and free-flowing.

Heather says there's an innate sense of knowing an arrangement is done: "When it looks right," she says, "I know it's ready." Till that sixth sense kicks in for the rest of us, we can fall back on spinning bouquets around to seeing if there are any gaping holes. In the end, Heather says that—beyond welcoming the outdoors in and basking in its beauty—working with flowers constantly reminds her that it's not us but Mother Nature who is in charge.

Place a few blades of local grasses, variegated pittosporum cuttings, and sword ferns sprigs in bud vases, and you've created a host of simple bouquets. Cut the woody stems on an angle, then slit or mash the ends so they can best soak up water. If cut straight across, the stem base will rest on the vessel's bottom and water intake will be impaired.

RESOURCES

Here's how to find the people and places mentioned in previous chapters, plus select information on the locations where we shot the photos.

INTRODUCTION

Hampton Park
At Rutledge Avenue, Cleveland Street, and Mary Murray Boulevard
Charleston, SC
843.724.7327 or 843.958.6435

CAMELLIAS

Kristin Newman Designs
Charleston, SC
843.723.6301
www.kristinnewmandesigns.com
Wedding designer Kristin donated camellias for this chapter, and later lent her azaleas, calligraphy talents, and miscellaneous props to the book's cause.

PFE Photo
Charleston, SC 29412
843.345.9190
www.pfephoto.com
Peter Frank Edwards gave this book its gorgeous photos and his garden's camellias, too.

Magnolia Plantation and Gardens
3550 Ashley River Road,
Charleston, SC 29414
800.367.3517
www.magnoliaplantation.com

Middleton Place
4300 Ashley River Road
Charleston, SC 29414
843.556.6020 or 800.782.3608
www.middletonplace.org

DAFFODILS

Brent and Becky's Bulbs
7900 Daffodil Lane
Gloucester, VA 23061
804.693.3966 or 877.661.2852
www.brentandbeckysbulbs.com

Cades Cove
Great Smoky Mountains National Park
107 Park Headquarters Road
Gatlinburg, TN 37738
865.436.1220
www.nps.gov/grsm

Camden Daffodil Festival
P. O. Box 693
Camden, AR 71711
870.836.0023
www.camdenfestival.com
Two days each March

Carnton Plantation
1345 Carton Lane
Franklin, TN 37064
615.794.0903
www.carnton.org

Cypress Gardens
3030 Cypress Gardens Road
Moncks Corner, SC 29461
843.553.0515
www.cypressgardens.info

Gloucester Daffodil Festival
Two days each March
6467 Main Street
Gloucester, VA 23061
804.693.2355
www.gloucesterva.info/pr

AZALEAS

Bellingrath Gardens and Home
12401 Bellingrath Gardens Road
Theodore, AL 36582
251.973.2217 or 800.247.8420
www.bellingrath.org

Magnolia Plantation and Gardens
(see Camellias)

Shore Acres Plant Farm
11545 Bellingrath Highway
Theodore, AL 36582
800.332.8197 or 251.973.1602
www.saplantfarm.com

Summerville Flowertown Festival

Summerville Family YMCA
and the Flowertown Festival
Administrative Offices
140 South Cedar Street
Summerville, SC 29483
843.871.9622
www.summervilleymca.org/flowertown
One weekend each April

ROSES

Boone Hall Plantation
1235 Long Point Road
Mount Pleasant, SC 29464
843.884.4371
www.boonehallplantation.com

Hampton Park (see Introduction)

Texas Rose Festival

Tyler Rose Museum
420 Rose Park Drive
Tyler, TX 75702
903.597.3130
www.texasrosefestival.com
The third week in October

HYDRANGEAS

Atlanta Botanical Garden
1345 Piedmont Avenue, NE
Atlanta, GA 30309
404.876.5859
www.atlantabotanicalgarden.org

Hampton Park (see Introduction)

Penny McHenry Hydrangea Festival
Douglasville Welcome Center
6694 East Broad Street
Douglasville, GA 30134
800.661.0013 or 770.947.5920
www.pennymchydrangeafestival.com
The first weekend in June

ZINNIAS

Landreth Seed Company
60 East High Street, Building #4
New Freedom, PA 17349
800.654.2407
www.landrethseeds.com
*"Seedlings" originally appeared as a blog
entry by Barbara Plantholt Melera on
the Landreth Seed Company website.*

Thackeray Farms
Harts Bluff Road
Wadmalaw Island, SC
843.559.9058

SUNFLOWERS

Gilliam Sunflower Trail & Festival
Red River Crossroads
Historical Association
P. O. Box 159
Gilliam, LA 71029
318.296.4303 or 318.296.4393
*Flowers generally bloom along Highway
3049 north of Shreveport the last two
weeks in June. The festival typically
is the last Saturday in June.*

Thackeray Farms (see Zinnias)

Rosebank Farms
4455 Betsy Kerrison Parkway
Johns Island, SC 29455
843.768.9139
www.rosebankfarms.com

Shoot Location

Page's Thieves Market
1460 Ben Sawyer Boulevard
Mount Pleasant, SC 29464
843.884.9672
www.pagesthievesmarket.net

GREENS

Shoot Location

Private home
Charleston, SC
Interiors by M Designs
843.834.0053 and Nest 843.568.2568

Out of Hand

113C Pitt Street
Mount Pleasant, SC 29464
843.856.3585
www.shopoutofhand.com
*We sourced wrapping paper
from this charming shop.*

GATHERING, CHOOSING VESSELS, AND ARRANGING

gathering: floral + event design

507 1/2 King Street
Charleston, SC 29403
843.723.3387
www.gatheringevents.com

GENERAL RESOURCES

Charleston County Public Library

68 Calhoun Street
Charleston, SC 29401
843.805.6930
www.ccpl.org

Charleston Horticultural Society

46 Windermere Boulevard
Charleston, SC 29407
843.579.9922
www.charlestonhorticulturalsociety.org
*Great talks and information on
Southern blooms and greens.*

Judith King

www.hydrangeashydrangeas.com
*Southern-based national expert
on hydrangeas with a wonderful
website loaded with information.*

SHOP SMART

Many local flower farms—even the ones that don't typically open their fields to the public—sell blooms to hosts, hostesses, and brides who need event-size orders. Some even grow small crops of specialty blooms for such customers, and occasionally farmers offer floral arranging services, too. Check with local farms to see what's possible in your area because not only is buying locally a great way to save dollars, it's also the best way to showcase what's of-the-moment fresh. Contact your county extension office for a list of nearby farms or visit these websites: www.localharvest.org or www.pickyourown.org

ACKNOWLEDGMENTS

CHARLESTON EDITING, PHOTO, AND STYLING TEAM

Especially Nicole Noble (who was a craft queen, too), and Lauren Brooks Johnson, Anna Evans, Bryan Hunter, Piper Monk, Pete Rerig, Mary Ruth Tribble, and Josh Zoodsma.

PLANT IDENTIFICATION ASSISTANCE

Miles Beach, Louise Bennett, JoAnn Breland, Ruth Knopf, Joan McDonald, Maarten van der Giessen, and Kathy Woolsey.

GARDENERS AND FLOWER DONORS

Louise Bennett, Boone Hall Plantation, JoAnn Breland, Charleston Lowcountry Rose Society, City of Charleston and Hampton Park, Cypress Gardens, Peter Frank Edwards, Tom Johnson, Sidi Limehouse, Joan McDonald, Magnolia Plantation and Gardens, Kristin Newman, Ruth Knopf, Shawn Thackeray, Jane Waring, Laura Waring, and Kathy Woolsey.

LOCATIONS AND PROPS

Eda Bigner (whose home, accessories, and generosity give new meaning to the term "mother lode"), Michael and Alison Brewer, Richard Ellis, Jenny Miller, Linda Page, and Fred and Judy Reinhard.

BACKGROUND

Steve Bender (via Southern Living), Charleston Horticulture Society

(and national flower societies), Bill Finch, Judith King, Nellie Neal, Ralph Null, Annie Owen, Felder Rushing, Sara Van Beck, and Jim Wilson.

SOUTHERN STORIES

Gordon Boogaerts, Serena DuBose, Eleanor Ilderton, Ed Johnson, the late Penny McHenry, Barbara Plantholt Melera, Pamela Smith Harriss, and Oliver Washington III.

PERSONAL

Melissa thanks Pete Wyrick for calling. Caroline Ilderton, whose story about her mother's camellias inspired the book. Her mother, sweetheart, family, best pals, many mentors, and Melinda Monk for their ever-flowing feedback, patience, and support. Lese Corrigan for making the introductions that opened the gates to so many Charleston gardens. And the production team at Gibbs Smith for their truly amazing eleventh-hour magic.

Heather gives special thanks to her mom, who instilled in her an appreciation for flowers and beauty. Her dad, who taught her the importance of hard work. Kristin, who always inspires her to reach farther. And Mary Ruth for her great company while "making it happen!"

Frank sends thanks to Sandy Lang, who always makes sure that some of whatever's blooming in the yard fills the house.